POETIC PRESCRIPTIONS
FOR
PESKY PROBLEMS

KATHERINE NORLAND

**Poetic
Prescriptions**
Publishing

Poetic Prescriptions Publishing
Katherine Norland
PO Box 17033
Encino, CA 91416

© 2008, 2020 by Katherine Norland

ISBN: 978-0-9983952-2-7

Photos and Cover Art: RT Norland
RobertNorland.com

Other titles written by Katherine Norland:

*Poetic Prescriptions for Eternal Youth: Examining
Earthly Beauty from a Heavenly Perspective*

*Poetic Prescriptions for Plaguing Problems: Biblical
Remedies for When Life Bites*

For more information, please visit
PoeticPrescriptions.com.

POETIC PRESCRIPTIONS
FOR
PESKY PROBLEMS

KATHERINE NORLAND

Acknowledgments

I'd like to thank my dad, **Donald**, who passed on to me his love for writing and taught me to keep plugging away like the proverbial inchworm. My mother, **Arlene**, who not only sacrificed by supporting me for years as I worked to fulfill my dreams, but also continued to love me even when I acted unlovable.

I am grateful for my husband, **Rob**, without whom I would have been stuck in a 9-to-5 job instead of being able to stop and write whenever the inspiration struck me.

Special thanks to my Sunday school teachers, **Pamela** and **Bob** Henkelman, who planted valuable seeds, and Pastor **Greg** Stone who watered them, supplemented by Pastors **Mel** and **Desiree** Ayres who taught me to be bold for the Lord.

Endless gratitude needs to be expressed towards the late **Marshall** Ferguson who picked me out of a crowd of people, encouraged me, showed me how to love myself, and coached me for many hours, sometimes through lots of tears. He convinced me to pull my poetry out from my personal "catacombs" and dust it off to show it to the world. He was the major contributor to my resurrecting the dream of writing that I didn't know even existed. . .until now.

And to **Timothy** Oman who helped me with my creativity on this second edition, and **Vincent** Galli for his precision in my wording and how it looks.

Most importantly, I thank Almighty **God**, the Originator, Author, and Finisher of my faith!

Author's Note

Poetic Prescriptions for Pesky Problems was the first poetry collection I ever published. Most of the poetry in this collection was written between 2003 and 2006, and was first published in 2008. I've looked back fondly over my first attempt at sharing my poetry with the world, and found joy in letters I'd received from poetry lovers and believers who, after reading, let me know how it had moved them. I didn't know much about writing poetry at the time, except that I loved how it sounded and how it made me feel. My heart was bursting with messages I wanted to share, and poetry seemed the perfect way of expression for me.

As the years passed and my love and study of poetry grew, I started to think I wanted a second chance at my first book. I wanted to keep the simplicity of what I had written, from a more innocent time of my life, before I had much life experience or children. I wanted to give it a fresh outlook for where I am today, after growing in my relationship with God and advancing a bit in my writing skills. I wanted to take the heart of what I had to say, and say it in a way that was more succinct and clear for my readers to understand.

This second edition of the book has been completely redone. Only one poem out of 77 has been left untouched. And I've swapped 14 of them out for 14 completely new ones, so it truly is new and improved.

I hope this new perspective on an old favorite suits you, and that you enjoy this fully updated version as much as I enjoyed the process of rewrites and going back to revive my first works.

Live True, Love Hard, Shine Bright,

Katherine Norland

Contents

I THINK I GET IT, LORD!

WHAT HE HAS DONE

RUN THE COURSE

YES, YOU CAN,
WITH GOD'S HELP

Let Go and Trust

I think that I can navigate
And know the best steps I should take
But when I judge by sight and sound
I'm more than apt to choose the fake.
> I'm blind and don't know where to turn;
> I keep on standing in the dark.
> With God I'll have a "fast pass" drive
> So why remain here, stuck in park?

That's why I've got to live by faith
And not make choices by my sight
Refuse the strongholds that I've held
Since they've been choking me so tight.
> Convinced that I am in control,
> My life's secure here in my hand.
> Yet there are countless mysteries
> I've yet to know and understand.

I try to plan my future well
Yet there's uncertainty and stress.
But God says only trust in Me;
Give Me your cares; I'll do the rest.
> Whenever I give something up
> And I replace it with what's right
> What held me in a headlock firm
> Will lose its grasp; its might gets light.

And then the more I'm in the Word
And without ceasing, kneel to pray
When times of testing come to me
It's not so hard to walk away.

And then the things that I once loved
And everything I thought was gold
Are not important when compared
To treasure from the Maker's mold.

Then when I'm linked in with the Lord
I can become more than I've dreamed.
Soon, swiftly moving mountains won't
Be far-fetched as it once had seemed.
  Whatever trials that come my way
  I'm confident God's got my back.
  With armor on, I'll lift my shield
  And wield my sword against attack.

God shall provide me everything;
He meets my needs and isn't done.
How could I even think to doubt?
For me, He gave His only Son!
  I'll let it go and cast my care.
  When I'm in prayer, I'll share each weight.
  I've read His Book, so I can rest.
  My trust in Him secures my fate.

God Knows What I Face

I'll not betray the same old way;
My past is cleansed and washed away.
The cross wipes out the dung I've done;
He loved me, so He sent His Son.

The future's planned; I need not fret.
And yes, He knows about my debt.
My state of heart's His main concern,
And Heaven's gift cannot be earned.

He loved me when I still was lost.
For me, He's paid the highest cost.
His blood washed clean my cankered sin.
I've shed the past and now begin

To live my life the way I should.
Discount those charging me no good,
I'll forge ahead, follow the plan
Confide in God; He understands.

There's nothing that He hasn't faced.
He's done it all and borne my place.
I'm standing firm, no need to pace.
I'll rest; my God knows what I face.

Only God Knows

God only knows where futures lead.
He only gives just what we need.
We say, "I know what's best for me,"
But not compared to what He sees.

He'll lead us where we haven't been.
We'll need more faith to go there, then.
We think, "What's this to do with me?"
He knows our callings to the nth degree.

Learn all we can, right where we're at,
There'll come a time when we need that.
God's blessings become manifold
When we are able to be bold.

God knows about our situation;
Let's trust Him with anticipation.
He'll make it better than we can;
He always has a higher plan.

I'll go with God and trust in Him;
God knows what we should add or trim.
When I'm in charge, I suffer lapse;
I'll step aside and shut my trap.

You Can Become
What You Thought You'd Be

The thoughts inside your heart and you are one.
Whatever thoughts you think, you will become.
There is a purpose; God has not "forgot"
His promise, though your life appears to rot.

For dreams to come, at times it's up to us.
We must surrender, offer up our trust.
Faith is the substance now of things hoped for.
That faith will manifest our dreams for more.

According to your faith, be't unto you.
Just need a bit, a mustard seed will do.
You've all authority, no thing to prove.
Command those mountains without doubt;
     they'll move.

You're given here dominion over Earth.
God cares for sparrows. Haven't you more worth?
He'll not forsake or leave you to the end.
More than a brother, He's a closer friend.

You will accomplish what you dream and more.
God's Word believed, will bathe you to the core.
Reflect now on His Word both night and day,
'Til all contrary thoughts have gone away.

Now ask, then you'll receive, and knock to find.
But most imperative, renew your mind.
Since as a man thinks in his heart, so's he,
You can become the one you thought you'd be.

Big Boss Has a Job for You

Big Boss rolled outta bed today
And outta all the things he knew
He needed workers in his field.
The harvest's plenty, workers few.

Weren't lookin' for those big degrees,
Those MENSA smart, them MBA's.
Just those who'll hunker down and work,
Who'll simply trust him and obey.

He don't care 'bout your references;
Ain't gonna be no background check.
Roll up your sleeves and get to work.
Don't mind that sun there on your neck.

Big Boss don't want no perfect folks,
Just honest kin who don't mind dirt.
Your fluffy titles won't help none.
Back-breaking work will make you hurt.

So if you're honest as the day
Is long, he's seekin' out pure hearts.
Stop standin' there just chewing hay.
Put on your overalls; let's start.

Don't worry none 'bout equal pay.
From His front stoop he sees you sweat.
He keeps on tracking ground you till
Someday you'll have your share; you bet.

He'll bid you to the farmhouse now.
You've worked hard like you were the least.
You'll sit down to the best home-cooked
All-country fresh, all-fixin's feast.

That day you'll meet him on his porch
When all the harvest has been won.
He'll pour a glass of lemonade;
He'll crack a smile and say, "Well done!"

Lead Your Sheep

You may not know just what to do,
But trust in Him; with God you can.
You may not know which way to go,
But trust in God's eternal plan.

You're set apart; you're made to lead.
The shepherd loves and tends his sheep.
You'll learn the means along the way.
Let God's precepts be those you keep.

You will not need the answers now.
He is a light unto your path.
Be on the lookout for the wolves
And love your lambs with rod and staff.

You may mess up along the way.
Take heart; you'll grow; you'll live; you'll learn.
Just keep your heart massaged with grace.
A servant leader's what they yearn.

In order to command a flock
You need some confidence and skill.
But if you don't believe you can,
Well then, nobody ever will.

Have Faith After I Pray

He'll do His work on time, and He'll not hurry.
My faith after I pray will triumph worry.
There's nothing that I've got He cannot cure.
He'll aid me to remove what isn't pure.

Alone I'm weak; I know I must rely
Upon the One who sets the low on high.
He is my remedy; my pain's decreased.
Release my cares to Him and troubles cease.

He must do what He says; He cannot lie
Which gives my faith the substance it was shy.

Rejoice

You say rejoice, now's not the time to weep?
I'm bouncing on the promises He'll keep.
I can't rejoice; the answers come too slow.
The process speeds when you've a seed to sow.

But if I plant, then my needs won't be met.
What's planted multiplies, so more you'll get.
You say rejoice before it comes my way?
It's not yours when it's seen, but when you pray.

For when you prayed, the answer had been sent.
Have patience waiting, trust and be content?
A battle rages stopping my rewards.
Sometimes it's held up by demonic hordes.

You say rejoice, to dread do not succumb?
Then soon the war is won, and answers come.
Soon burdens are removed by heav'nly hoist.
Keep praising 'till I've reason to rejoice?

Keep praising 'till you've reason to rejoice.
I praised until I'd reason to rejoice!

Showing God's Love to You

My Daddy wants to show His love
He even lets me help sometimes
He lets me cheer some people up
Long as I'm back before bedtime

When I sit down and share my lunch
It makes some people cry with joy
I pat them on the back when sad
When bully Satan takes their toys

No, I don't mind it none at all
See, I got lost once at the store
I know what scared is like, okay?
But you don't have to cry no more

Sure, Daddy knows you need a bath
He knows you got some owies too
He'll kiss your boo boos when you fall
His love is big and wide for you

When no one wants to be your friend
When they don't pick you for their side
No, you don't have to feel alone
'Cause He picked you and He won't hide

He's gonna wipe away your tears
Just like a puppy licks your face
No, you don't need to worry none
He don't care if you broke a vase

I promise, it will be okay
Get up; let's go and meet my Dad
His name is I Am; He don't change
And He will make your heart feel glad

Now grab my hand and hurry up
My Dad will make you feel brand new
You wanna join my family?
He's got enough love for you too

Pre-Season Game

On the sidelines the Great Coach stands
His strategies will be revealed
Take heed of His game plan to win
And schemes become unsealed
You've played well in the scrimmages
Adept defensive player
Now brush up on your offense
And be a demon slayer

Now keep your head here in the game
Your thoughts can't wander 'round
Before you're trusted with the ball
Must learn to take some ground
Do not despise your training time
Or needed practice drills
For strength and stamina are gained
You'll need them climbing hills

You gotta listen to the Coach
Things aren't exactly what they seem
He knows which tactics will be used
By the other team
Your muscles scream and you're all sore
It's not what you would order
And yet this training camp is good
To fly through that first quarter

Keep up the pace with game face on
Yo, this thing ain't a scrimmage
You'll tackle all opponents since
You're made in Coach's image

Just know the scouts are watching you
In this pre-season game
So, help your teammates also shine
Don't look for your own fame

Know all positions on the field
Defend and pick and run
This is your championship game
You're not just here for fun
The Coach's game plan cannot fail
So, play what you've been shown
You're guaranteed the victory
You're dancing in the zone

Be a Soul Winner

You're blameless now; don't bring your sins
right back.
Don't chew the devil's words; it's an attack.
Repent, and then dwell on your sins no more.
God doesn't keep your nice or naughty score.

We're not in bonds; we're not oppressed.
God gave us freedom; do what's best.
Tell all you meet about the King
And show them love, the highest thing.

Our tests are testimonies now.
You're set free—you can show them how.
We went through trials for a reason.
We're the salt; let's be the season.

So, sprinkle truth, but use some grace.
Keep flavor fresh; don't lose your taste.
Don't crave acceptance; take a stand.
Is Christ your secret? Bloody hands!

This is your chance; don't bite your tongue and wait.
The urgency has never been so great.
Let's win the souls of doctors, friends, and dates.
Share Jesus with them, ere it gets too late.

CAN YOU HEAR ME NOW, LORD?

Show Me You

Help me build the habits needed to succeed.
Keep me from the snares that might
    slow down my speed.
Power me with wisdom; knowledge is the key.
Take me from this pit to where I need to be.

Grant to me Your patience when I can't hold out.
How do I forgive when I just want to pout?
Give me all the love You have for wretched fools.
Bring to light Your secrets, centuries of clues.

Show me only You! How is't that you're so kind?
Utter all to me; I'm begging; move my mind.
Show Shekinah glory; turn my drab hair white.
First I must surrender, not put up a fight.

I Thirst

I thirst for Your knowledge; I thirst for Your truth.
I thirst to break chains of bondage
obtained in my youth.
I thirst for Your wisdom; I also thirst for Your grace.
I thirst for humility, the kind You had
to take my place.

I thirst to hear Your voice; I thirst for understanding.
I thirst for Your patience;
don't want to be demanding.
I thirst for the confidence to ignore the persecution.
I thirst for Your love that led You to the execution.

I thirst for Your strength to stand against the devil.
I thirst to come up to You, not stay at man's level.
I thirst to be gentle to children,
humbly change diapers.
I thirst for conviction to boldly drive out
the "brood of vipers."

I thirst to be about my Father's business, not my own.
I thirst to calm the waves of the sea
and the wind-blown.
I thirst to see the sick healed and the lame walk.
I thirst to see blind eyes open and the mute talk.

I thirst to carry the truth to all who'll hear it.
I thirst to receive admonition and not fear it.
I thirst to lead the unsaved away from slaughter.
I thirst to lead the thirsty to the Living Water.

Before

Before I talk to mortal man
I need to talk to You
Before what's in the frying pan
Your bread of Life's consumed

Before my morning coffee hit
I'll drink the Living Water
It makes my lazy brain more fit
And balanced without totter

Before I've got to start a task
My knees should hit the floor
Make You my number one to ask
And make no choice before

Meanwhile . . . On Earth

I sit and think what life's about
Well water's deep; I'm in a drought
Alone I can't; my failures prove
My strength won't make these mountains move

I yearn for more. What do I do?
To get breakthrough, try something new
Be patient, how? I'm getting old
I've many stories to be told

'Til timing's right, how will I fare?
How would You say I should prepare?
I shy inside and stay at home
While marketers blow up my phone

What are the fruitful doing now?
Time leveraged, hired hands push plows
Is what I'm doing even right?
Give me a sign, to keep my fight

My time is being spread so thin
No stamina, the shape I'm in
I'm tired; my will is nil to follow
I'm just a shell—inside I'm hollow

I feel no joy; I know I should
I was secure in where I stood
'Til swayed by those I thought knew more
Their half-baked truths have left me poor

Speak to Me

The utmost thing is when my Savior speaks
I seek to drop my tasks; my interest peaks
But yet, I'm nervous hearing His decision
What if I execute without precision?

I sorta want to hear; there's much at stake
Too soon I do what makes His huge heart ache
I'm desperate for His answers when I pray
But what if I've no will to live His way?

You're making sure I'm safe; you're watching me
Renew my mind to see the way You see
I do want You to speak, yet I have fear
You're going to say what I don't want to hear

What You'll speak holds more weight
        than worldly fact
If I don't heed, I'll perish from attack
I've got to trust You'll not be a killjoy
Enrich my vision, spotting each decoy—

That hinders me from what I'm called to do
So, speak to me; I've got to hear from You
Please speak; I squinch my eyes and hold my breath
Your Words give life, transporting me from death

Harvest Breakthrough

The stack of charities
To help is piling up.
But how can I pour out
If I've an empty cup?

When is my harvest here?
You know I need it now.
So many here to help.
My bank account shouts, "How?"
I do put others first,
And it defies my reason.
I do believe Your Word.
My present is "due season."

I'm glad to do Your work,
And yet I need assistance.
I too have bills to pay,
And here I face resistance.
I'd like to fund the gospel,
Helping those in need.
I'd like to oust from me
What's left of any greed.

Long died to my old flesh
Until it resurrects
That old dirt bag must stay
My spirit You'll perfect.
I'd like to lend a hand
When people are in pain.
I'll channel all my coins
Where they'll get Godly gains.

Into the gospel plant
I go to save the lost.
To God, all life is dear.
He paid the highest cost.
So what can I hold back
Compared to God's great coffer?
I give 'til I've none left.
I'm ridiculed by scoffers.

"Where is your bitty portion
God's Word has bragged about?"
How can I keep my faith
And pulverize my doubt?
God give me patience now.
What is it I should do?
"Shh!" He says. "Sow your seed
'Till harvests break on through."

How can that be it?
What else could I do?
"Shh!" He says. "Sow your seed
Till harvests break on through."
But God, there's no return.
Is there another way?
Until your harvest comes
Sow! "Shh!" Is all He'll say.

Resting on the Wire

I don't want to waste my time
But tell me where to draw the line
I don't want to slip down hills
That You have called me now to climb

I have a sneaky human mind
It justifies most selfish things
And yet I want You pleased with me
And all the offerings I bring

How can I quiet down my brain
When time has come to take a rest?
When toiling on, I've done too much
Help me relax and not protest

It seems I over-analyze
Nitpick each detail far too much
You slow me down, put me at ease
My pulse abates with Your kind touch

Not mine, but Yours, prioritize
Complete, cross off what You say do
And rip the rest from ragged list
A world of guilt won't help me through

I've got to breach the finish line
Push past the herd at starting gate
Don't stay in lazy haze, make haste
No laurels won if I am late

I see the wire; I fix my eyes
I'll score the cup, but You're my prize
I'll run with everything I've got
I rear and wait to hear the shot

Child of the Divine

I'm overcome by Satan's blitz
When sleeping or awake.
But in my humanness, how can
I strike back where it aches?
Please silence out each voice
Delivering defeat.
I trust You heard my plea;
I need not repeat.

Please hold me in Your mighty hand,
So there's no way to slip.
I know I should be mindful of
Words slipping from my lips.
For we shall have what we declare.
It's written in Your Word.
I'm comforted that You're aware
Of every single bird.

And how much more will You step in
Providing for my need?
A wealthy Father showing up
Each time at perfect speed.
And though I often make a mess;
At times I botch my task.
And yet You help to make repairs
When I have humbly asked.

You are divine; You've called me child,
And it's by choice, not chance.
I've learned I've lived beneath my rank,
Beat down by circumstance.

Was blind that my adoption meant
My parents are the Trinity.
And all Your children are an heir
In Your divinity.

Your children do not beg for bread;
You know our hearts' desire.
And You don't mind if now and then
I have things I admire.
There's no place I can't boldly go;
You said the earth is mine.
Reclaim the earth from Lucifer
Oh Child of the Divine.

To Get a Breakthrough

Something is festering, pestering me.
Is it Your glory, Lord, coming to be?
What do I do? I stand here lost, confused.
I want to win, not lose. What do I choose?

Each day I lived in urge to serve You, Lord.
It pays to give away what I afford.
Yet at my peak I'm weak, like standing still.
I'm not so strong. How long is this here hill?

I duel without fuel, no relief in sight.
I lie here, Lord; make sharp my sword to fight.
I stay and pray; I know You hear my prayer.
Freshen my faith, so I don't question if You care.

It's rough to feel I'm not doing enough.
If I do different stuff, You tell me, "Shush."
"There's always more to score in earthly life.
But steer from others; lend ear to my advice.

Nothing to prove to make me move your life.
It's apparent, you're a good parent and wife

I'll tell you what to change and rearrange.
Make prime your time with Me; don't be estranged.
'But what now, Lord?' you ask,
with sword held steady.
Your hand in mine will make
your stand more ready.
You want the best to manifest here and come to be?
For new breakthroughs, spend extra time with Me."

Help Me Be the One

My Master, help me be the one
        Whose actions match Your Blessed Son's
The pastor asked of God and cried
        My sheep, on me they have relied

To lead them on to that pure light
        I'm charged to show them what is right
I cannot veer or steer from You
        I'm judged on all I say and do

I cannot bear to let them down
        You set them free when they are bound.
My Master, help me be the one
        Whose actions match Your Blessed Son's

To step in, when they've desperate need
        I'll try my best to take the lead
He wiped sweat from his brow and said
        My flock, they must be warm and fed

I'll put my congregation first
        I shouldn't have to be coerced
Avoiding pride and arrogance
        Apologies tear down offense

My Master, help me be the one
        Whose actions match Your Blessed Son's
Let mercy, truth, and grace flow through
        Make me a line that leads to You

If someone's hurt, I'll help, not sit
      Won't be that idle hypocrite
A megachurch is not my goal
      But growth of their eternal soul

I won't be fixed on my own hurt
      Though Satan's left me eating dirt
My Master, help me be the one
      Whose actions match Your Blessed Son's

Rest, Relax, and Renew

How come You always seem to move so slow?
Why don't You pick me up when I feel low?
I'm overwhelmed and don't know where You are.
I search for You. How come you are so far?

My plans abound, I have such lofty goals.
You said it's possible; You'll foil my foes.
Things closing in, I'm feeling claustrophobic.
Some greater reason why You seem to hold it?

Hold what? My future, blessings, harvest, prize.
Where is Your knowledge? You can make me wise.
But people trample, smash me to the ground.
They mock: "Is your God nowhere to be found?"

The years add up, all while I slowly cook.
Can't see Jehovah Jireh, yet still I look.
How long must I stay trudging in this rut?
Should not You love me still, no matter what?

No answers found in counsel, though it's righteous.
When there's no help, deciding that I must just—
Take time for bits of rest and relaxation.
Quit forcing myself into this vexation.

My "problem solver" crashes when I'm tired.
Fatigue makes all look bleak, and life is mired.
Elijah slayed each false and lying priest,
But fled the evil queen filled by the beast.

The angel fed him, forced him into rest.
Elijah needed shade to do his best.
I must remember when in my earth suit
I can't do all; I'll need me some recruits.

Drop pride and ask for help whene'r I need it.
Don't wait until I'm empty, then to feed it—
Feed what? My inner man, can't just eat bread.
But all of God's words—power to raise the dead!

I THINK I GET IT, LORD!

You Perfect Me

Write my name in the palm of Your hand. Count
every hair on my head. Work all things together for
my good, according to Your purpose.

Delight in the prosperity of Your saint. You who
spared not Your own child, freely give me all things
that pertain to life and health. Perfect until the day of
Christ Jesus, the good work You began in me.

Supply all my needs. . .
according to Your riches in glory
    through Christ Jesus
Strengthen me. . .
and make my feet like the feet of a deer
Qualify me. . .
to be a partaker of the inheritance of the saints
    in the light.

Give me rest and protect me under the shadow of
Your wing. Establish me and guard me from the evil
one. Lord, deliver me from every evil work, and
preserve me for Your heavenly kingdom.

Justify me by Your grace so I can become an heir
according to the hope of eternal life. Make
intercession for me. Lord, take away the first to
establish the second. Forever perfect those who are
being sanctified.

Be faithful. . .
to those You made promises to
Reward those. . .

who diligently seek You
Exalt me. . .
in due time when I humble myself.

Be my helper. Give me every good and perfect gift
from above. Because I believe in You, never allow me
to be put to shame.

Be not slack concerning Your promises. Be my
advocate with the Father and the propitiation for my
sins. Because I believe that Jesus is the Son of God,
help me overcome the world.

Rebuke and chasten me. . .
because You love me
Send the Holy Spirit. . .
to give me comfort and power
Fill me. . .
with Your fullness.

Give me an irrevocable calling, and gifts. Grant me
according to the riches of Your glory, and strengthen
me with might through the Spirit.

Do exceedingly abundantly above all I ask or think
according to Your power that is at work within me.
You hold the future in the blink of an eye, and the
whole world in Your hand. Don't let Your blessings
stop.

A House Made of Broccoli

Don't allow sin to draw you in;
of course it's attractive.

Hansel and Gretel wouldn't have been drawn in
to a house made out of broccoli.

They were drawn into a house made out of candy.
That way, the witch could get them
and put them in the oven.

What's before you may smell and taste superb.
Sin always looks appealing,
but it will kill you!

Katherine Norland

Forwarding Address Requested

Dear Friend,

I really need to spend some time with you
But I have family life and things to do.
I fear I don't have time to even write.
I hope you don't think I've been impolite.

It's hard to finish what I want each day.
It seems the time just slips and slips away.
But I've no idea where that time does go.
It's all for naught, if naught there is to show.

Before the house awakes, I read your letters.
I know I should respond; I will be better.
You've expectations of me that I drop.
Perhaps I waste my time and let it rot.

Last time you paid a visit, you were irked
Since I was comatose and overworked.
We sat there by my fireplace in peace.
You said this life of mine was just on lease.

You wanted to relax out in the yard.
You told me I'd been working far too hard.
You said I love you just the way you are.
You've other workers doing your PR.

I said, "How can I rest? There's work to do."
You said, "So what? It doesn't bother you."
And that you've got an army helping out,
Your hand on mine, there's more to talk about.

Remembering that day has made me smile.
I thought I'd write; I know it's been a while.
I can't use busy-ness as my defense.
You've more to do than me; that makes no sense.

You pause it all to keep me on Your grid
Although You care for billions of kids.
I'll work and rest enough, but I won't whine.

P.S. Please write me back, if You have time.

Sincerely, your friend, Kat

The Mind Is the Battlefield

This smoke, it burns my eyes
I'm helpless to see clear
Debris from bombs lays waste
How could my goals be near?
Here, there's a pressing force
That aims to keep me down
And water can't be tread
I may give in and drown

Lethargically I lie
Like clay that cannot move
There's carnage everywhere
I've no strength to remove
My eyelids, heavy tombs
I've fallen to despair
Now I don't care to war
I vegetate and stare

The hours seem like years
As I disintegrate
My goals here turn to dust
Wind blown down steel grate
Not many battles won
Yet Satan picks on me
'Cause he sees what I can't
He flies the heavenlies

When God clears all the smoke
He takes away nightmares
There's worship in my heart
You heard my foxhole prayer

Now joy fills me inside
A glimmer hits my eyes
I'm closer to my goal
Than I had realized

But Satan knew that fact
He tried to make me quit
And he used every trick
So I'd give up on it
If I had known my foe
And his misguided fleet
I wouldn't be so quick
To yield or to retreat

In truth, he can't stop me
Just tell me it's too tough
Whatever it will take
I haven't got enough
Yet now I know the mind
Is where he will attack
So I won't quit the fight
But rather battle back

Evict Them

I'm moving to the side Divine
So I can get ahead
Must toss out all my excess bags
And do it without dread

A minimalist I'll be, for
That's easier to carry
Why haul around what harms my heart?
Let live what I had buried

I will not be a packrat since
I've learned it's detrimental
Or take the bed bugs when I move
For they're not paying rental

I've boxes full of harmful things
All stacked up in my mind
I've got to send them packing now
There's freedom I can find

Evict unwanted visitors
Eject what's left behind
Make room for where You're taking me
The digs that You've designed

The Best Spread Secret

Psst! I've got a secret; I can't speak too loud
Get close so you can hear me; you're allowed
I know this guy; he can get you what you need
If in the slammer, he can get you freed

He knows the judges; he can pull some strings
Get you acquitted, many other things
The mob's harassing you; just say the word
And don't keep quiet; sing it like a bird

Listen, I'll get you in on somethin' big
A sure thing, I'll cut you in on this gig
He's lookin' for a partner in his plan
It's foolproof, in demand by every man

So do you want in on this mystery?
This guy controls the cosmos; he's with me
A limited-time offer, whadya say?
This family's yours, if you want in today

You meet my boss; you'll be part of the crew
You'll get a pass, won't be no cement shoes
Don't be a wise guy; there's 'nough to go 'round
His name is Love, the best-spread secret found

Our Problems

I get depressed and void of hope
My thoughts then go astray
Then realize that I forsook
My time with God today

Oh, sure I've read my Bible and
I spouted a quick prayer
My heart is confident in that
The Spirit of God is there

Yet I'm lethargic and appeased
I need to get excited
My spirit and the Lord's must link
Again become united

I know He's in my heart and He
Will never go away
But caught in tumult of this world
I often lose the fray

I must move quickly, not to skip
Our close relationship
The longer that I'm gone, I slip
And cannot hold my grip

When I commune with God, I have
A more sure-footed traction
Then my desire to lie around
It gets replaced with action

Non-sensical ideas I have
Like leeches on my brain
Are ripped and thrown into the sea
They shrivel and I'm sane

Come right into His circle; don't
Just teeter 'round the rim;
He's overcome the world and so
Have we, if we're in Him

The reason we have problems is
Away from God, we've shoved
Our problems all arise because
We don't think we are loved

More Suitable

With only half obeying God
I don't obey at all
Then when my battles must be fought
I wonder why I fall

God told me what to do and yet
I only do a part
I *know* I know what's best for me
I'm set apart in smarts

I'm cool. Why follow all those rules?
It's fools who don't behave
My Maker wants to save me but
I'm digging my own grave

Could my way be more suitable
Than His? He knows the end
Why do I think that I know best?
I can't see 'round the bend

Get Out of Your Way

I should just get out of Your way
It's clear my answer's always nay

I rail, complain, and feel so hurt
When You have been so hard at work

Arranging heaven and the earth
To let me know how much I'm worth

When I'm a fool and lose my faith
You still fill up my empty space

Pretending that the good from You
Is earned because of what I do

Learn patience when You tell me stay
And kindly get out of Your way

Grow in Me

Grow in me, Your planted seed
More of You will meet each need

Give me wisdom to abound
I need discernment to be found
And knowledge more than I could gain
Your healing power cancels pain

I need Your love to pass around
Your freedom when I'm trapped and bound
Your heart that's warm when mine is frozen
Opens doors when mine are closin'

Grow strength in me when I am weak
Your character is what I seek
I need Your help when in too deep
Your mindfulness on what to keep

Need boldness going where You call
Your grace to brace me from sin's fall
Your eyes of love to look at others
To lend forgiveness to my brothers

Grow peace in me when times are tough
Provision when there's not enough
Approve me when I've been rejected
Send angels so I'll be protected

Your shoulder when I need to cry
Salvation, meet me in the sky

From the Head to the Heart

I've done all that I know to do
And yet that's just a start
God, help me quickly move Your Word
From head down to my heart

Your Word received can make me free
It gives the good report
And gets my proud flesh to subside
It shows where I fall short

You are perfecting me each day
I need it every minute
If I have no encouragement
The race? I couldn't win it!

You've given me the handbook, but
I must make time to read
Most times I think that's good enough
But next I need to heed

Verbatim, I have memorized
Your Word, but don't believe
So all the good You have for me
I never will achieve

It's not Grand Canyon in the size
That keeps us far apart
It's only eighteen inches from
My head down to my heart

Declaration of Guilt

Oh, here I go again; I found
A dozen things to do
Before I sit to meditate
And spend some time with You.
I say You're my priority,
But I don't seek You first.
Relying on Your grace, and think
That I can act the worst.

And it's all dandy fine until
Things start to go all wrong,
And then with haste I run to You
With my defeatist song.
You fix it since You love me, but
I know You'd be more pleased
If setting my first hour aside
To spend it on my knees.

I thank You, Lord, for being there
And cleaning up my mess,
But if we had communion first
I'd need the clean-up less.
You show me what to do and where,
And what I should avoid.
If I were You and saw my wreck,
I'd wholly be annoyed.

If it were me in charge, this place
Would be a big disaster.
I don't think there is anyone
Who could destroy it faster.

Whip me in line, kept into shape.
You've got to chastise me;
It's what I need so I'll become
What You want me to be.

And at the rate I'm going wrong
I must have some assistance.
My spirit's willing, but my flesh
Keeps putting up resistance.
I may not have complete control
Until the day I die,
But now and here, I'll try my best
To make my flesh comply.

Resides or Presides

Yes, He resides in you
But must preside in you
For we will be transformed
When God's laws are performed

His Spirit dwells in us
To kill our flesh—we trust
Infusing us with power
Our spirits reign this hour

Then He won't just reside
In us, He must preside

WHAT HE HAS DONE

It's Selfishness, It Seems

Without You, all is lost. And what's the point
of dreams?
If living for myself, it's selfishness, it seems.
Aspiring to do so much that makes me smile,
Yet now I question if my goals have been worthwhile.

I slug it out, make vision boards for inspiration,
And yet I've found I'm lacking in the aspiration.
If every day's a battle, without You, it's not won.
It's not worth waking up, if there were not Your Son.

If striving for a goal, but You are not involved
It isn't long before I find my drive dissolved.
Your sinless sacrifice was offered on the cross
For moldy, sinful me, with heart encased in moss.

But You rip clear away all things You didn't plant.
I give my earthly life, eternal You will grant.
So I've exchanged the dreams I found were vanity
To use my heart's desire to help humanity.

Without You, there's no point; without You, all is lost.
Saw past my wicked acts and said,
"She's worth the cost."
If living for myself, it's selfishness, it seems,
So I will live for Christ, the granter of my dreams.

Ask

The mountain-forming God reveals His thoughts
    to man.
The infinite invites us in His splendid plan.
If we seek answers and we do what He would ask,
He'll teach us to complete and conquer every task.

He's never hiding from us; He's right by our side.
When we don't know the way, He's ever glad to guide.
Can't be just curious; won't find Him if we're peekers.
Be serious—He's found by unrelenting seekers.

You're standing at the side door, wailing
    that it's locked.
The door would swing wide open if you'd only knock.
So don't throw in the towel, and just get irked
    and leave.
Hold to the towel, then in His name, ask, and you'll
    receive.

I Am a Willing Vessel

I am a willing vessel now;
I didn't used to be.
But now I'll be the first in line
Insisting, "God, use me!"
Lord, not my will but Yours be done;
I've said this all before.
But now it's true, and I believe
I want it more and more.

I've pecked at doing things my way.
This bird would really hurt
To see them fall and flatten out
My failures hard at work.
And yet, I'd load my back and flap;
Can't soar with heavy loads.
I'm grounded doing things my way;
I kick against the goads.

My back is broken, feet are bruised
When I go my direction.
When following Your path, I'm safe;
For You are my protection.
When targeted by hunters then
I'm camouflaged in peace.
I'll fly Your way from here on out
Until my life does cease.

No, it was never easy when
I did it my own way.
But now I have the Lord with me,
So come whatever may.

So keep on filling me till full
I'll stay in Your shalom
A willing vessel pouring out
Until You take me home.

Speak as God Speaks

My arms are raised; I praise and dance,
'Cause God is in my circumstance.
When all is lost, I'm down to nothing.
Here, I can trust He's up to something.

I cannot comprehend it all.
He holds me up, so I won't fall.
Old fears still whisper, "What's to come?"
I don't begin until God's done.

God knew my path since my beginning.
When holding God, I'm always winning.
I'll have whate'er it is I say.
I've learned from Jesus how to pray.

He called things out as if they were,
With confidence and peace assured.
My words reveal what's in my heart.
What target's hit with each word dart?

God spoke the world into existence.
Not one atom gave resistance.
Since we're a chip off the old Rock,
Let's talk the way that He would talk.

Forget about the devil's threats.
God gave us power that makes him sweat.
If we're in Him, we are complete.
The devil's found beneath our feet.

If Satan wants to speak to you
Then tell that loser what to do.
To leave that note of lies, he'll spew
Beneath the bottom of your shoe.

Tossed, Scattered, and Confused

I'm scattered and confused; I don't know
    where to start.
Emotions toss me 'round like waves, rip me apart.
I'm toiling all in vain; His presence has been missed.
Agendas filled by stress, disjointed to-do list.

Your presence is so sweet; I never want to leave.
My head and chest do rest; it's onto You I cleave.
Coherent are my thoughts, for You make all succinct.
I mustn't move from here; can't chance a broken link.

I love this peace of mind and how You've filled
    my heart.
I'll tether close to You, so we will never part.
When I connect with You, I have an overflow
Of all I'll ever need for what I'll undergo.

Expectation

I've raised the level of my expectation
Because my Lord gave me the invitation.
Said, "Test me now and see if I am good,"
So I don't have the need to "knock on wood."

He'll pour out blessings that I can't contain,
That Wall Street won't be needed to maintain.
And I'll bless others, since I have been blessed.
Each time I do, it makes more manifest.

When to and fro, I've gas enough to go.
My needs are met by all the seeds I sow.
Yes, I'm unstoppable; I have no lack.
My sacrificial seeds fight off attack.

I'll praise Him with my lips and too my heart.
He knows that's where my treasures do depart.
I know God's plans are best; He has a reason,
So patiently, I'm waiting for due season.

He gave me all my strength, so I don't cave.
And that's why more of Him is what I crave.
Whatever He allows is what I need.
He graces me to move at lightning speed.

I'm with You, Lord; go on and count me in,
With expectation higher than it's been.
In currency, it says in You I trust.
When You my deed co-sign, I can't go bust.

God of the Impossible

My God is good, yes, all the time!
He ceaselessly surprises me,
As everything He touches turns
Out better than I thought it'd be.

My furrowed brow of worry rests;
I'm unconstrained and overjoyed.
And all my worst scenarios
That plagued my thoughts have been destroyed.

Yet faced with the impossible,
When harrowing assaults have come,
I'm apt to panic more than pray
Like all is lost and I'm undone.

Ah, then God does the "couldn't be,"
Performs astonishing results,
Obliterating each attack.
All Satan's schemes screech to a halt.

Then soon I'm feeling crummy guilt
Because my faith had been so little.
Yet God brings me a supple strength.
I cannot break, no longer brittle.

The God of the impossible
Makes sure my battles all are won.
All things are possible for me.
The number of excuses? None!

The Real Cure

You're versed in all my thoughts and all my ways
My plans are oft dim-witted
When Satan charges me for my offense
You make sure I'm acquitted

When people do speak ill of You, and talk
Through lips of ignorance
My testimony and the lamb's shed blood
Will be my best defense

You're my supporter, ally; You provide
Both fortress and a friend
You always come to my defense. How could
Your name I not defend?

You heal what ails me; You're my advocate
You save me from my trial
You lead the way, don't always carry me
Yet walk with me each mile

Of popping these placebos, I am tired
When You're the honest cure
Remove my dross; refine me in Your fire
So all that's left is pure

God Keeps Blessing Me

My God, He keeps on blessing me,
Yes, more and more each day.
And I've not earned all of the gifts
He freely sends my way.
    The spirit in me leaps.
    The joy I feel's so deep.

I cannot keep this feeling in;
I'm laughing all the time.
The Holy Spirit makes me soar
Much better than fine wine.
    It's hard to sit real still
    When you are Spirit-filled!

His blessings are too much for me;
I've got to pass some on.
I never fear that I'll run out;
His stock is never gone.
    When opening my hand
    The gifts He gives are grand.

When we receive with open hands
Enjoy what is for you
Then we're not apt to close our fists
But give like God does too.
    If hoarding's what you wrestle
    Then learn to be a vessel.

Must stop the stockpile of your stuff
Possessions grasped so firm.
It won't rise with you when you die
But go down to the worms.
> When giving, you've no lack.
> Much better will come back.

But if you only want the things,
There's something that you've missed.
The Giver should be Who we seek
And not what's on our list.
> He fills us when we ask.
> The world's within our grasp.

And though He wants to give us much
Not if it costs our souls,
We must take stock, weigh honestly
Priorities and goals.
> Let life be more than stuff,
> For God alone's enough.

Cheshire Cat Grin

My joy is spilling out; it cannot be contained.
It mucks up grumpy grudges; it is unrestrained.
I have untold abundance; here I overflow.
A solar flare exploded due to Whom I know.

My spirit's jubilant; from bliss to bliss it leaps.
I cannot touch the ground; the clouds
        are where I sleep.
Click, click, click, click, tap dance on rainbows just for
pleasure.
Oh no, it's not because I have success past measure.

When people gawk at me and my Cheshire cat grin,
Announce to all who'll hear, I've been redeemed
        from sin.
It's like ten thousand choirs of angels fill this place.
No wonder I can't wipe this smile off my face.

When people say, "You're glowing. What is it
        you do?"
I know I'm glass and it's God's light
        that's passing through.
Unfettered joy awaits, and Cheshire-cat grins too.
So liberate your smile; it's so long overdue.

THANK YOU, GOD

Change

It's strange that I've been changed
By the One Who stays the same.

The Same inspired this change in me,
Tore off my scales so I could see.
You hoist my head, give me good posture.
In me, You placed good things to foster.

You gave me strength against my foe,
And boldness so I could say no.
And friendships torn, You help me mend.
Now wish life would extend, not end.

And here I live without regret.
Pain of my past I now forget.
All changed when I bowed to Your name.
Life conquered and won't be the same.

The One Who stays the same
Has strangely left me changed.

Rest Cozy

You seem so burdened by your dream
It is but something you must bear
Believing it's God's will, keep on
That He delights to answer prayer

You have been faithful; that He sees
Let fear of missing out release
With God, you can have any dream
Take joy; rest cozy in His peace

Choices of Animals

I make bad choices acting on instinct.
You save me so I won't become extinct.

I am endangered; You want me preserved.
You guide Your scattered sheep into Your herd.

You throw me bones, although I chase my tail.
My speed is perfect, though I'm just a snail.

My grip won't slip when swinging from these trees.
I swelter in this fur; You're my cool breeze.

It's no mirage; You are my wat'ring hole.
You help me see, although I be a mole.

Can I store water like a camel's hump?
If ponds are wet, this frog can really jump.

I'm in a fix, bare paws on hot tin roof.
You give nine lives and make me fireproof.

I eat from dumpsters, making dumb mistakes.
A cold-cut stray, although you offer steak.

With head cut off, I'm on a chicken run.
Icarus moth, I fly into the sun.

I fly highways to find what pleasures me
And end up roadkill in the first degree.

Like pigs, I roll in mud; with that I'm facile.
I dwell in squalor; You would grant a castle.

I'm trained in loyalty, to sit and stay.
When I obey, You keep the fleas away.

I was a stubborn mule who wouldn't shift,
But now Your Child, and Heaven is my gift.

So parent me, an heir to Kingdom's throne.
I'm not a beast; I have your chromosomes.

Thanks and Praise

Thank You, God, for making me bright.
Thank You, God; Your timing is right.
Thank You, God, for giving me peace.
Thank You, God; my troubles have ceased.
Thank You, God, for helping me fight.
Thank You, God, when nothing goes right.

Thank You, God, for sending Your Son.
Thank You, God; Your doing is done.

Thank You, God, for unending grace.
Thank You, God, for showing Your face.
Thank You, God, for taking my sorrow.
Thank You, God, for lighting tomorrow.

Praise You, God, for joys yet to come.
Praise You, God; there's no other One.
Praise You, God, when I laugh or cry.
Praise You, God, when I fear I'll die.
Praise You, God, for hearts that You mend.
Praise You, God, for mercies no end.

Praise You, God, for talents given.
Praise You, God, for You are risen!
Praise You, God; I leap like a deer.
Praise You, God; I've no need to fear.
Praise You, God, for enemies mine.
Praise You, God, for constancy Thine.

You've taught me well, Your truth and Your laws.
You've shown me love, no matter my flaws.
You've helped me live, to go on each day.
I'm humbled now; I'll seek and I'll pray.

My God, My God

My God, my God, You are my El Shaddai.
I can't run low because You're my supply.
My God, my God, with whom could You compare?
You answer yea and amen, every prayer.

My God, my God, You sent Your only Son.
I start in faith and it's already done.
My God, my God, You cause me joyful tears.
Your boundless love, it casts away my fears.

My God, my God, so endless is Your peace.
I trust Your Word. Who needs to lay out fleece?
My God, my God, redeemer of my time,
Absolving and restoring me from crime.

My God, my God, Whose judgments are correct,
I'll take what You may give, and not inspect.
My God, my God, You help me through each goal.
My God, my God, the holder of my soul.

No Grumbling Allowed

Why did the Israelites walk forty years?
Were they ungrateful, leaking pity tears?
Were moaning and complaints what made them slip?
And stretch to decades long, a two-week trip?

No, grumbling won't get you from here to there,
Except where you don't want—it's called a "snare."
You'll have a cloud above, so march and smile.
You will not starve; the Promise Land's worthwhile.

It's possible to get one hundredfold
If we're obedient in what God's told.
So keep your joy, though you've no leeks for stew.
His blessings far outweigh what you've been through.

Do I Dare Ask for More?

Almighty God, do I dare ask for more?
Still hungry, though I know You've filled my stores.
I'm bent; I'm not content with what I've got,
Although You've turned my bit into a lot.

There are a few more teensy-weensy things
I'd like to pretty-please ask You to bring,
Like words of wisdom, so I'm not a fool,
And faith to use my sword when in a duel.

How 'bout the gift of miracles and healing?
Discern the spirits, know just what they're feeling.
Oh, and those "tongues divers" for when I pray,
Interpretation, knowing what I say.

When will I get the gift of prophecy
To see that spirit-realm activity?
I want more knowledge, so I'll understand.
I hope You don't take this as a demand.

Could I have more desire to reach the lost?
Remove my selfishness to pay the cost.
And let me be a leader, not just follow,
Prescribing truths that may seem hard to swallow.

Ah, scratch that last request; may be too hard.
I'd rather not leave hearers burned and scarred.
Let's face it, Lord, I'm sometimes way too rude,
Aggressive, argumentative, and crude. . .

Annoying, jealous, lazy, know-it-all,
Conceited, thoughtless, bossy. (Watch me fall!)
I'm spoiled, tactless, crafty, and uptight,
Compulsive, disobedient, ne'er do right.

I'm grumpy, nervous, cynical, defensive,
Complaining, carping. I am blunt, offensive. . .
A smarty-pants who interrupts when hurried,
Unpleasant, inconsistent, clingy, worried.

I know I often come off as a brute.
Yeah, maybe I should ask for Spirit's fruit.
Oh, I know! How about more love, less hate
To stop my lashing back when I'm irate?

I need more patience; I can't wait,
More joy when things aren't going great,
More peace when I am shaken up,
More self-control when time to sup. . .

More goodness, which makes others glad,
More kindness when I'm treated bad,
More gentleness—help me be meek,
More faithfulness. It's You I'll seek.

Well, maybe this has been a test
And I should trust You'll give what's best.
I need You most, not what You'll bring.
If I have You, I've everything.

Doing My God Job

Our calling's urgent since this place is fading.
The enemy's soft words now loud and grating.
Be real to me; I'll brace for persecution,
And sentence this, my flesh, to execution.

I was afraid to rush into the flame.
I feared a burning if I spoke Your name.
But threat of scalding will not hold me back.
The devil's done enough; now I'll attack.

By leading those to God in His control,
My goal: no soul will crash against the shoal.
With Your protection, I don't dread the mob.
I'll be a witness, doing my God job.

I'll do my work with diligence and joy.
I'll pull the needy onto this convoy.
I'll lead them all to You; I'll be Your tool.
Now guard my mouth so I don't speak a fool.

I pray my conduct and Your Word align
So that I never cast my pearls to swine.
You say to seek Your wisdom, not mere man's.
And though the waves may shake, make wake;
    I'll stand.

I'm in this lifeboat, laboring with zeal.
I toss the lost, the buoyant Savior's wheel.
The world dies, yet we see that beacon shine.
We're saved from shipwreck by the light Divine.

Ain't Ruin No More!

Some once-upon-a-time stories are truth,
So let me share one 'bout Naomi and Ruth.
It'll take a piece, so git ya a chair and sit.
Jus' bide yer time; this tale of love is gooder 'n grits.

Now, I'm not sayin' Naomi was old,
    but to make it clearer
It was as if Methuselah was starin' her in the mirror.
Ruth, purty as a sack o' puppies,
    was her daughter-in-law.
Mahlon was Ruth's husband,
    and Elimelech was his pa.

But let's back this tractor up and find out
    how it came to be.
Ruth lived in Moab, on the east side of that
    dead old sea.
The Big E (Elimelech) and Naomi, they were wed,
    lived in Bethlehem.
That famous little town is where
    their family had stemmed.

Now, nestled in the south side of them smokey
    mountains of Judea,
A cattywampus trouble was a-comin',
    and they had no idea.
Naomi and the Big E, they had some young'uns,
    two sons.
They named one Mahlon and the other Chilion.

But there was dag-nab famine; it had gotten real bad.
They had to fish or cut bait, so escaped out to Moab.

Naomi and Big E's boys grew from youth,
And "Chili" married Orpah; "Malie" married Ruth.

But their pa, Big E, he had gone and died.
Naomi stayed with her boys and their brides.
And then, not long after, by some queer turn of fate
Both boys had dropped like flies and left their mates.

Now, if that don't rattle your bones and put 'em
    on a grill,
Naomi howled like a banshee, left poor
    as a whippoorwill.
Naomi done did hear she'd find vittles in Judah
So her daughters-in-law and her went for. . .yeah.

Naomi felt guilt to have the girls stay, but she
    weren't about to beg.
"Go on; watch out fer the marsh rabbits;
    they might take off yer leg."
Naomi was gonna throw herself a stank-as-a-skunk
    pity party.
They wailed like a 'possum passin' a porcupine,
    real hearty.

Now Orpah ran like trapped and scaled dog,
    who'd been sprung,
But Ruth—sweet and loyal, silly-as-a-goose Ruth—
    she clung.
Naomi said, "Go on, git! You're young;
    find another mate.
Even if I had more chitlins right now,
    you wouldn't wait.

'Sides, I'm too shriveled up and old
    for a child to grow."
But like a mule is stubborn, Ruth refused to go.
"I'll go where yer a-goin', sleep where yer a-sleepin.'
Yer folk'll be my folk; Your God, I'll be a-keepin.'"

Naomi said, "Gitcha sum smarts," but
    Ruth was headstrong.
Seems now Naomi had a hitch in her git-along.
So they left, uprooting Ruth from her hometown,
    Moab.
They schlepped in gunny sacks to Beth'lem
    what little they had.

Now, in them thar hills of Bethlehem, the whole town
    was a-stir.
They whispered loud as a cat in heat, "Naomi?
    Could that be her?"
Naomi thought they was high as a Georgia pine,
    with all their chitter,
And answered, "Call me Mara, now, for God made life
    so bitter."

They said, "Why you mad as a hornet, like all has
    gone awry?"
Naomi spouted back, "I'm so down; I'd have to git
    better to die."
"My boys done kicked the bucket 'fore their ole ladies
    bore some young.
If y'all wanna throw rocks, believe me,
    you'll git stung."

Then, hotter 'n a hen on a hot rock, they left those
    chumps.
Naomi told Ruth, "Life is simpler when you plow
    around the stumps."
How the twain would make a wage would be a feat.
Two can live as cheap as one, only iff'n one don't eat.

Naomi had turned into quite the cantankerous broad.
That Ruth musta been thinking, "Don't git yer
    knickers in a wad."
Ruth said, "I'm fit as a fiddle; my strength
    won't wane.
No skin off my back. I'll hit the fields and glean
    some grain."

See, harvesters in those days couldn't gather all of it.
They often dropped down some grain, and so
    she'd git a bit.
When the field owner, Boaz, saw Ruth,
    his heart did yield.
He said, "Little missy, stay and glean; don't go
    to any other field."

"You hungry hound dogs, don't lay a hand on her,"
    he told his men.
And Ruth found favor as easy as fallin' off a log then.
Boaz said, "My friends call me Bo, and to me
    it's been made known
You left yer cozy double-wide to treat Naomi
    like yer own...

You'll have a rich reward for what you done."
With ole Bo's kindness, Naomi's heart,
    'twere overrun.

Bo asked Ruth, "Didja eat yet?" She shook her head.
"Y'wont to?
It'll cure what ails ya. Take off a load,
and join my crew."

That feller, Bo, was whipped, and might tryin'
to win her.
"Whoo, doggies!" Bo proclaimed. "Winner, winner,
chicken dinner!"
She sat with his threshin' workers, eating
roasted grain.
It jarred up her preserves, a-wonderin' if he'd
be her swain.

She ate till full as a tick on a hot-blooded hound dog.
She were wallowin' in her mind, happy as a hog.
See, that feller, Bo, was not a-wantin' Ruth to leave.
Told his crew, "Let her gather grain from 'mongst
the sheaves.

Pull out the stalks from bales, and drop 'em
on the ground."
She gleaned without their tongues a-lashin',
all that she found.
She carried back more than any gleaner would,
a massive share.
When Naomi saw the haul, she pert neer fell
from off her chair.

Naomi said, "Where'd ya glean; where was ya
workin' at?
I been to a goat rodeo but ain't never seen nuthin'
like that."

"Boaz was the name of the kind and gentle manfolk,"
    Ruth said.
Naomi shook her head: "He's kind to both the living
    and the dead.

That man's our kinsmen redeemer,
    and part of our clan.
Don't corner nuthin' meaner than you;
    stay with this man."
Now fer those of ya ain't never heard of a kinsman
    redeemer 'fore,
He's simply a man of kin, related by blood,
    who had a chore. . .

Like buy back a relative's property, avenge the tribe,
    do his share,
To redeem his dead kin, like marry his widow
    and provide an heir.
Now then, the word *redeem* is to purchase back,
    liberate, rescue,
Or take our sin and sufferin' like the good Lord did
    for me and you.

Naomi was tougher than a one-eared alley cat,
    rough as a cob.
And she would git their ducks in a row; Ruth
    would keep this job.
So, Ruth stayed like white on rice to Boaz's ladies
    while she gleaned,
Until the harvest was all hauled in, and the fields
    picked clean.

Don't be antsy none, think this tale ain't worth a hoot
    and a holler.
I ain't yet got to the good part that'll crack yer yaller.
Naomi, salt of the Earth, wanted Ruth
    to be provided for
So she said, "Tonight, Boaz will be on threshin' floor."

Naomi continued, "Listen to yer elders; I know
    what's best.
Git out them high-water britches, wash and
    perfume yerself, wear a dress.
When the wee hours come, hide away, and just
    let him drink and eat.
Wherever he hits the hay, you lay, and then
    uncover his feet."

Stop yer gigglin. Exposin' his hooves, 'tweren't
    some weird way to show affection.
Nope, then it was an act of submission, asking
    for provision and protection.
Fer them who're still confused, I'll fix yer thinkin'
    so ya knows:
Unwrappin' callused dogs of his, was how Ruth
    was to propose.

So, Ruth got all gussied up and did all Naomi
    said to do.
She watched that feller, Bo, for hours, eat, be merry,
    and drink his brew.
A watched pot never boils, thought this water'd
    never thaw.
But soon Bo was plumb tuckered out, and snorin'
    like a saw.

Then Ruth, she creeped in all quiet-like, and gave
    his cloak a tug.
Curled up next to his bare tootsies, snug as bug
    in a rug.
Ole Bo, alone, felt empty as last year's bird nest.
    Ruth never knew.
Like a cat lickin' a grindstone, he startled awake,
    "Who are you?"

She said, "I am your maidservant, Ruth;
    please cover me.
You're a guardian redeemer to Naomi's family."
Now when she said cover me, it meant like protection
    under a bird's wing. . .
That he'd take responsibility, make her his wife,
    and give offspring.

Bo said, "Bless you, my daughter; you've shown
    more kindness than before.
You didn't run after younger men, whether rich
    or poor.
You don't need be a scaredy cat, but in
    my kindness bask.
Oh noble, virtuous woman, I'll do all you ask."

Bo lay like a bump on a log, thinkin' "How do you like
    them apples?"
Right thar and then, he wanted to haul her off
    to the chapel.
He was a-scratchin' his head, not sure how he'd
    explain
That there was another closer kin in the family name.

"And if this kin wants this duty of redeemin', I must
  see to it.
If not as the Lord lives, I'll work like a beaver,
  and I'll do it."
Ruth was so shocked; she was knocked into
  next week with delight.
See, 'tweren't fittin' back then that a Jew
  would marry a Moabite.

Ruth held back; she wasn't gonna be all over him
  like a cheap suit.
She didn't want no folk thinking she was a woman
  of ill repute.
See, Ruth had taken on a big risk in doing
  what she did.
There was a room full of people who could wake up,
  God forbid.

Bo said, "No soul can know you were on
  the threshing floor.
If a woman be found to stay the night, it would cause
  an uproar.
Ya gotsta make like a tree and leave, 'fore yer
  seen around."
He gave her a bundle of barley and soon
  set out fer town.

Ole Bo said, "Iza gonna go git me sompin'; I be back."
Ruth said, "I'll be over yonder, d'reckly, jus'
  waiting at my shack."
We'll I'll be—Ruth did what Naomi asked,
  laid it on the line.
And now this waitin' business, it took too much time.

Naomi said, "Good Lord willin' and the creak
    don't rise,
Ole Bo'll settle this today. Go on and dry yer eyes.
You're cryin' noisy as a pet 'coon; it's frightnin'.
Rest, Ruth; he'll be back faster 'n greased lightnin'."

Ole Bo found the nearer kin redeemer; they soon
    sat down.
Bo, wantin' to getter done, he grabbed ten elders
    in the town.
Boaz said, "Naomi is selling the land of Elimelech.
Yer the closest relative, so you git first pick."

The closer kin said, "If'n you'd be more sp'cific, 'bout
What yer askin,' I might be able to help you out."
Ole Bo spun the tale of how Naomi had come back
And told him if he didn't want Ruth, He'd pick up
    the slack.

Well, Ruth sat home neat as a pin, a-wonderin'
    if she would marry,
And why ole Bo was slower than molasses in January.
Ruth, fidgetin' at home, waitin, was harder 'n
    wrestlin' gators.
But jus' hold yer hats; this gits gooder 'n salad,
    better 'n taters.

Ole Bo said, "You buy the land and Ruth but
    must also maintain.
Your child will take on Big E's family name."
That closer kin turned red as a pickled beet,
    thinkin' of that trap.
Said, "I need to redeem that, like an airplane
    needs mudflaps.

I can't, never could do nuthin' with that tree trunk
    o' weight.
Like grease on glass doorknob, it be slippery
    to my estate.
Yer askin' me go ta skinny dip with snappin' turtles.
    Would *you*?
With that whopper-jawed request, when pigs fly,
    I'd say yes to you.

Oh, Bo, that's like pushing a watermelon through
    a garden hose.
That request is bigger than a barn, and I gots to say
    no's."
Bo said, "You got more no's than I can
    shake a stick at.
You ain't been sucked through a knot hole; didn't
    no one skin yer cat.

No need to beat a dead horse; yer using a cannon
    to swat a fly.
Pull up yer britches and quit whinin'; it don't make
    no never mind."
Now, back then 'tweren't enough to make a deal
    just with words.
Bo can't count his chickens 'fore they're hatched;
    he had no bird.

No, back in them there times, there was an old
    tradition they'd do:
To make transactions bindin', you'd have to give
    your shoe.

Katherine Norland

Bo said to that kin, "I see you did bring your shoe,
    withya, didja now?
I'll take the bull by the horns; you don't have to
    give up yer cash cow.

I ain't trying to convince ya o' nuthin', if it's more 'n
    you can handle."
So, front of the elders, like a bat outta hell, that kin
    gave Bo his sandal.
That's how they made a public record in Israel,
    God's honest truth.
Givin' Bo his sandal meant he gave up rights
    to the property and Ruth.

Bo thought that kin was crazier than a loon,
    but he didn't care.
He won the lotto with Ruth; she was as fine
    as frog's hair.
Then all the elder witnesses gave their blessings
    to ole Bo.
On the way home, he shook his tail feathers,
    and he had a glow.

Bo left that thar meetin, struttin' like a rooster
    with a grin.
That closer kin's attitude was uglier 'n homemade sin.
He ran to Naomi's, lickety-split, and grabbed his
    honey bun.
Bo took that fine filly Ruth for himself, and
    they conceived a son.

Naomi, Bo, and Ruth had no idear how far their bond
    would reach.
I spun this yarn fer y'all 'cause the best sermons are
    lived, not preached.
The women of town said to Naomi, "Praise be, t
    he Lord.
God saw you came in ruined, but
    He made you restored.

That Ruth is rare as hen's teeth, better 'n seven sons.
You'll be sustained in your old age; God isn't done."
Ruth bore a son, and they named him Obed.
Naomi cared for him, then all her bitterness
    was dead.

When growed, Obed, their boy, begat one, Jesse,
    David's dad,
Whose kinfolk begat Christ, our Kinsman
    and comrade.
The story's moral is: trust what yer Maker
    has in store.
Life might leave you a-weepin', but
    you ain't ruin no more!

Such a Time as This

You're wondrous, as you're made by His design.
Like Esther, you've a mission that's divine.

This is your time you've been made rightly for.
When God swings wide the door, there's good
    in store.
You're led correctly when you watch and listen.
He'll give you treasures that do more than glisten.

Cousin escaped the gallows by His grace.
Her courage spared extinction of her race.

His plans for you, alone you can't attain.
All that He has for you won't be restrained.
And just like Esther saved her generation,
It could be God made you to change the nation.

Perhaps your goals have made some people laugh,
And though the bigger goals are harder tasks,

The harder tasks mean you need more of God.
Why reach for things that you can do while flawed?
If you're to change the world, show them His light.
You'll need to gently lead in doing right.

Step uninvited to the King and plea,
Not knowing if you'll die by His decree.

That's why you must be purified to start,
Not just perfumed in oil but in your heart.
There will be persecution; you know that.
He knows what you can handle, where you're at.

Through you, God's perfect timing is displayed.
There was no better time to have you made.

You could keep silent, fearing, turn your face.
But God would send another in your place.
And all He had for you and yours, you'd miss.
He made you now for such a time as this!

BASIC INFO B4 LEAVING EARTH

Perfect Love

The couple fear and love won't coexist.
With fright I'm riddled. So what did I miss?

God's love is perfect, but I don't believe
I'm qualified or worthy to receive.
Why am I frenzied; what is going on?
Where is my steady faith that's Great Wall long?

Why fly apart when things don't go my way?
Why don't I trust what God's Word has to say?
It says don't worry—"No, I'm just concerned."
Pray for those who use you—"I'll get burned!"

Do not forsake assembly—I stay home.
If answers fill the Word, then trust His tome.
God says He will supply all that I need,
Yet I don't plant; instead, I eat my seed.

He'll hide me 'neath His wing; I could abide,
But fear of missing out keeps me outside.
I will not fight, for fear I'll be defeated.
There's more to life—I let myself be cheated.

I'm scared of everything and everyone.
Think if I follow Him, I won't have fun.
I brood about what people think and say.
It plagues my mind; so heavily it weighs.

All thoughts that torment me, I'll be free of.
My terrors cast out by His perfect love.

8 Questions

What don't I need to do?
Worry.
What causes most mistakes?
Hurry.
How can I get ahead?
Service.
What should I never feel?
Nervous.
How oft should we spend time?
Each day.
What's best for me to do?
Obey.
When will You quit on me?
Never.
How long will I be loved?
Forever.

Fruition Is When?

When nothing happens, I am still content.
To do what God has asked is time well spent.
And when the time is right, God moves me quickly.
If rushed, I may get caught in something sticky.
My talents will propel my destination,
Not chasing honors due to my frustration.

When God has made no effort to be early
That's when my faith will grow, so I won't worry.
He'll show up when He feels the time is right.
There's no real reason I should feel uptight.
When on the Cross, He said that it was finished.
I'll shine my light, not let it be diminished.

I'm being watched when I am in a trial.
If life's a mess, must handle it with style,
And operate as if my prayers came true
By thanking God for what He soon will do.
Just trust it's coming; I'll quit asking when.
I have it when I pray; fruition's then!

Meditate on These Things

My words most often taste of chimney soot.
My habit: open mouth and insert foot.
Yet conscientious people too have slips.
Abundant venom dropping from their lips.

Apologize, they may, with passion, say
"It wasn't me; I had a ghastly day."
Can't take it back and bear a brand-new start,
If but a sliver, it slipped from the heart.

You must take care of it. What should you do?
To voice good thoughts, your mind must first renew.
If it comes out, you know it first went in.
A heart of gold now turned from what was tin.

To dwell on toxic thoughts, you shouldn't say.
Will make dreams die and resurrect decay.
Watch out! Don't slip if you have lost your grip.
It's just in jest, you quip, but here's a tip:

Reflect on what is noble, true, and just,
All pure and lovely things; for it's a must.
If it's of good report or any virtue,
The notion's worthy; it will not hurt you.

These things that you have learned, received,
    and heard
When meditating here, your faith's assured.
Observe the good Paul modeled, and so do,
And then God's peace will always be with you.

Simplify Your Life

Why should you simplify your life?
It's good to do too much
When overworked, I'll steal your joy
And get you in my clutch
Keep complicating life on Earth
No time for God; you race
How else will you be bound for hell?
Keep going at that pace
                                        – The Devil

You're overloaded to the hilt
But status, fame, it matters
You're in commitments, buried deep
It's normal to be scattered
White space in datebooks? Wussie stuff
You're jacked and have no peace
So what? The wealth is worth it all
You'll rest when you're deceased
                                        – The World

Yet you fill your own calendar
And surely could see to it
If you don't want to do it all
Then you don't have to do it
Now write down everything you do
And all that you would like to
Inspect what bears the choicest fruit
And cut the rest out from you
                                        – The Author

Make time to spend with family
Don't always run; stay home
Go walk among God's garden's bloom
Relax and read a poem
God gives desires of your heart
Don't live a life that's hated
Go for your goals; get close to God
Enjoy what He's created

— The Angels

Take time to fellowship with folks
Don't hurry down life's path
Have pillow talk into the night
Hold hands and belly laugh
Start basking in the setting sun
Abandon work to play
It's time to simplify your life
And seek Me every day

— The Almighty

Remove Your Limitations

So far to go, my set point needs to be reset.
Recalibrate my goals to God's; mine are a threat.
Glass ceilings shattered, limitations are now nil
And dreams He placed in me, I can, I will fulfill.

Time passes by; no longer will I sit and wait.
I live in apathy; that's a pathetic state.
I won't stay here; it's not spiritual to settle.
I'll get involved with life; my duty is to meddle.

Be in control, take me off auto-pilot.
My focus flies precise; I thread an eyelet.
Prayers answered by the passion level you pursue.
You're not awaiting God; He's there, awaiting you.

God's not offended if we ask for far too much.
But He is if we think He can't do such and such.
Accept disease, defeat, or debt; it's compromise.
Stop living lower than God freely authorized.

When you decide you've limits, then you're saying no
To all God has for you, where He wants you to go.
Don't blame Him for your life when you've kept
        on the throttle.
All things are yours; let Abraham be your model.

Not just your muscles atrophy when not in use.
If you're not building up your faith, you've no excuse.
To rid our limitations, traits like these are key:
Your faith—must use it, to its full capacity.

Your diligence—the Word says it will make one rich.
Relationships—guard hearts; watch who
    you spend time with.
Your generosity—not hoard but give away.
Your holiness—for God is holy; we obey.

What if you were required to rid your limitations?
Would you be more effective, going to the nations?
Don't think that it's too difficult a thing to do.
Because the diligent obtain what they pursue.

Information vs. Revelation

Now meditate on Me, reflecting on My Word
And let it cancel out the so-called "facts"
    you've heard.
When first in Eden, we'd hold each other dearly.
We walked together and communed;
    you heard Me clearly.

You knew all in an instant; you had revelation.
Now you don't know much; it's all just information.
The age of information, can't survive without it.
So when you hear My voice, at once you start
    to doubt it.

It doesn't fit your research, or what
    you've been taught.
You wouldn't need to search if My words
    had been caught.
The knowledge learned from man is always based
    in fear.
You must do this or that, or tragedy draws near.

But that's not how I work; I have a simple plan.
My foolishness beats out all wisdom drawn
    from man.
What's taught by man is poppycock you'll have
    to sort.
When you commune with Me, your time to wait
    is short.

Good and Faithful Servant

I've given you nine-tenths. How will you use it?
On worthwhile living or will you abuse it?

The borrower is servant to the lender.
Why do you feel the need to be a spender?
Don't lay up treasures that can be destroyed
By moths or rust or thieves who're unemployed.

And who on Earth do you aim to impress
That you'd pay all that interest on a dress?
To government, a third of your pay goes.
God's covenant, a tenth, don't you suppose?

There's razzle dazzle that you want to get,
But is it worth the rising piles of debt?
You may give handouts when you see some beg,
But what's the future now of that nest egg?

Where are your savings for a rainy day?
It won't abruptly show up when you pray.
God gives much when we're faithful with our little.
Forsake your worldly lusts; begin to whittle

Away your debt; invest your time and pay.
When stewardship's been good, you'll hear God say:
"Well done, you've been a good and faithful servant.
Your talents were not buried; you've been fervent.

Increase came since you sowed the seed I gave,
Ignored commercial hype and didn't cave
Into the lure for what you didn't need.
It was My Word you chose instead to heed.

What you forgo in order to please Me
You'll get a hundredfold back; you will see."
When you make putting God first as your vow
You'll be blessed in eternity, and now.

Katherine Norland

Name It and Claim It

I can't live any way I please
And pray that God will bless it.
I can't get everything I want
Just 'cause I might confess it.
It's only when obedient
That all good things will follow.
Without God, even good things lack;
They'll all feel void and hollow.

It's best when God gives riches,
Those he adds no sorrow to
But if I want the things, not Him,
I haven't got a clue.
Though He supplies my needs, He's not
My private piggy bank,
Where I can draw out all I want.
Clean out that mind; it's rank.

No matter if I call it "faith"
Or else "name it and claim it,"
If void of God, I'll spend my life
Just trying to sustain it.
My duty's not to just call out
And say what He would say.
I'm also meant to walk in love,
To follow and obey.

I'll take the time to think about
Why I want what I want.
Is it to share with others
Or say I'm blessed, and flaunt?

I'm going to do a motive check
Before I "claim" a thing.
For only those with servants' hearts
Will be promoted king.

Help the Blind to See

If people don't know God, they're blind.
You must untie them from that bind.
Be brave; you've got a gift to give.
Proclaim His truth so they can live.

The great commission's what to do,
And what you plant comes back to you.

Our home on high, we'll be one day,
So we can't be afraid to say
I am His child, for whom He's died.
He's coming back to get His bride.

He brings me joy at every moment.
He is my Savior, so I own it.

Who cares what others think of you?
His will is what we ought to do.
He's coming soon to take His own
And bring them to their heavn'ly home.

Then we'll rejoice eternally
If we have helped the blind to see.

Walk in Love

I've found in life we all get hurt;
That's how the cookie crumbles.
Yet we must keep on getting up
When we've had trips and tumbles.

And people close to us can be
Our greatest cause of pain.
Let God be your umbrella; He'll
Protect you from the rain.

No matter all the nasty things
They said or that they've done,
You can't change anybody else;
You're culpable for one.

You'll be aghast at what folks do,
And they'll think that they're right.
We'll get upset and we'll forget
They're not whom we should fight.

We battle principalities,
The powers in heav'nly places.
And if we don't leave op'n a door,
They can't get in and chase us.

We can't be harboring a thing
Against our fellow man.
Yes, God forgives, if we forgive.
Let's line up with His plan.

What issues do you have with them?
What tartness do you stow?

When praying, ask that they be blessed
Until they're good to go.

You don't know if their lashing out
Is from some inner pain,
'Cause someone did them wrong, so they
In turn just do the same.

Look at them through the Father's eyes,
For they're the ones that see
Their hearts. Now say, "It matters not
What they have done to me."

We're called to love unlov'ble folks;
This is the place to start.
If we as Christians don't do that,
Then what sets us apart?

Then we're like those who don't know God
But bound by sets of rules.
Why give up pleasure, go to church?
We're just a bunch of fools.

If punishing folks for the deeds
They ignorantly do,
Should God be merciful to us
When we're a sinner too?

And like a serpent, let's be wise
Yet gentle as a dove.
What makes us different from the world?
It's when we walk in love.

RUN THE COURSE

One Will Have Regret

One stands inside the shadow, while
The other's in the light.
And yet they both have equal choice:
To do what's wrong or right.
This one walks on the winding road,
The other on the straight.
But both will face fork in the road
Where they will choose their fate.

The one likes to be catered to;
The other is a servant.
One trusts in his ability,
The other in prayers fervent.
This one appears to have it all,
The lot he's always wanted.
And yet he doesn't sleep at night
Since all his dreams are haunted.

The other's only goal in life
Is that God's will is done.
And he sleeps like a baby, sound
Which gives him strength to run.
One runs on outward stimulation
And perceived success.
The other runs on inward joy
And takes the time to rest.

One trusts his own financial strength
And still pops pills to cope.
The other's trust is in God's Word
And that gives him true hope.

The one works seven days a week
To keep up with his neighbor.
The other knows six days are best,
Then he must rest from labor.

The one neglects his own and friends
For monetary gain.
The other knows them closely, and
They share each other's pain.
Someday they both will meet their end;
Just one will have regret.
The one whose thoughts were "profit!" "loss!"
Forgetting his sin debt.

God Says; You Say

God says do this. You say, "Not now."
God says do that. You say, "But how?"
God says talk to them. You say, "What would I say?"
God says get this done. You say, "There's
    no time today."

God says give this away. You say, "It's my stuff."
God says pay their bill. You say, "I may not have
    enough."
God says give this person a ride. You say, "But
    there could be danger."
God says pray and lay hands on them. You say,
    "But they are a stranger."

You say please do this. God says, "Not now."
You say please do that. God says, "But how?"
You ask God to talk to them. God says, "What
    would I say?"
You say help get this done. God says,
    "There's no time today."

You say can I have this? God says, "It's my stuff."
You say please pay my bill. God says, "I may not
    have enough."
You say my car quit; I need a ride. God says,
    "But there may be danger."
You say take this sickness from me. God says,
    "But you're a stranger."

Stay

When having a distressing day
When you've no strength to even pray
When you run late and there's delay
When working long, no time to play

When problems can't be kept at bay
When stress makes all your hair turn gray
When bills are more than you can pay
When seeds you harvest sprout decay

When clouds obscure the warm sun's rays
When snow is bullying in May

When you can't make it through the day
When lethargy begs you to lay
When each request is met with nay
When nothing tried turns out okay

When you can't think of what to say
When no one hears you shouting, "Hey!"
When rushing to escape God's way
Then trust Him more; press in and stay

God's Burden Is Light

I don't want to cry; I'm only asking why.
I'm sick of feeling that I want to die.
I want to work hard, on my own to stand
But feel sometimes like I can't lift my hand.
I want to read but can't see through the tears.
I want to make the calls without the fears.
I want to cast out thoughts that paralyze,
To step up front in faith, become God's prize.

I want to see the way the Father does,
To take Him at His Word—yes, just because.
I always want to see the brighter side,
And never lose sight that I am the bride—
The Bride of Christ, and what more could I need?
To know God deeper, read and read and read
His Words to know just how He feels about me,
So, when failing courage blinds, I can see.

I know I can't do much; I shouldn't worry,
Embrace the journey sans the rush and hurry.
I don't have lazy fingers in my hands.
I'll quit accepting all the world's demands.
Because their standards make sure I can't win,
And then I spiral down and can't begin.

Thank God He doesn't use that kind of measure.
I need to do His will, which gives Him pleasure.
His will is not too hard or out of place
And if I make a mess, there's always grace.
I need not push uphill for every part.
It's His delight to fill my yearning heart.

So I can pick my head up every day.
My "Daddy" is a simple prayer away.
I'll try it now, and He'll give me His best.
The weak and heavy laden, He gives rest.
God's burden's easy and His yoke is light.
When walking with Him, it all turns out right.

No Regret

Sweet solace missed. Where's promised peace?
Unfurl those fears to bring release
These self-imposed false expectations
Derail before I reach the station

My goals, they laugh, "She'll reach the moon!"
I'm worse to me when I lampoon
I wait for goals I've never met
And dread the thought of life's regret

Get Out of Jail

> *Release yourself from your own prison*
> *Did you forget that He has risen?*

We're busy punishing ourselves
For all the things we don't do right
So then we let our guard go down
And aren't effective in the fight
A taskmaster demands perfection
When we track what we've done wrong
Which means our ears have been tuned in
To Lucifer's seducing song

His lucid lies make us believe
That we're not worthy to take hold
Of everything God has for us
And dance with God on streets of gold
He points out everywhere we're weak
And ways that we don't measure up
So, then we feel it'd be a sham
To drink from the communion cup

We've opened up to take their bane
And now they're haunting day and night
Recycling all our mental lists
Replaying all we didn't do right
We've pulled away from those at church
We're wretched sinners, far too guilty
Can't look the pastor in the eye
He'll see our lies and know we're filthy

Soon, we can't read the Bible's text,
Since it shows us where we fall short

"That's right," the hiss from Satan comes
"You're a screw-up" is his retort
Now we can't even look at God
We feel we're nothing but a failure
Locked away in prison's clink
We watch the beast become our jailer

And now we're trapped behind our minds
That slammer's stronger than steel bars
Replaying all our felonies
And misdemeanors that caused scars
He drives a wedge 'tween us and God
He nitpicks every indiscretion
Now too ashamed, we push away
From God before we've made confession

So, soon the guilt takes us by storm
And what we've done eats us alive
Then Satan brings his famished friends
They pick us clean; on fear they thrive
Yet God still tries to speak to us
He's always sending others too
But we've been chained up to the wall
And can't break free. What should we do?

Call out to Jesus; He finds joy
In setting captives like us free
He doesn't want us bound by sin
But as unfettered as can be
When Jesus took away our sins
He did for ones we've yet to do
Not just today or yesterday
The lies the devil brings aren't true

So, push away from Satan's table
Don't eat that fiend's most rotten rations
That canker-worm makes all good spoil
Feast with the King; He has compassion
For every lock, His blood's the key
When you've repented, you're pristine
There's freedom in the grace of God
You've been expunged; your record's clean

He set us free; get out of jail
He took the Cross to post our bail

March Forward

March? No, not me; I'll march nowhere
You'll send me places I can't bear
Your name's exalted on my lips
Yet to obey? Excuses! Quips!

Forgive the error of my ways
Instead of march, I'd rather stay
For You might send me to a place
Where they don't like my honky face

Like maybe to some Third World space
I'll be poked full of "vaccinates"
Contract disease that might be rare
March? No, not me; I'll go nowhere

Perhaps You shouldn't be so subtle
Or I'll rehearse all my rebuttals
Don't be afraid, says Your Good Book
I can't stand back and merely look

I shouldn't crave my comfort zone
You'll come with me to the unknown
Yes, You'll look out for my welfare
March? Yes, I'll march to anywhere!

He Has Begun a Good Work in Me

If saying "I can't," I know I surely won't.
Why do I pursue when God tells me "Don't"?
When eyeing problems, I think of defeat.
Why don't I learn? I let my fails repeat.

Why make mistakes that I have done before?
Why can't I trust that I'll soon be restored?
Why am I murmuring at God today?
He is the potter; I am just the clay.

Creation can't be sore with the Creator.
I'll cast my cares. Why must I wait 'til later?
He'll grant requests, yes even when they're small.
To Him, it's not too trite. Why do I stall?

There's not a problem, no, that is too great.
I must give those to Him, not hesitate.
He's got my back when I'm under attack.
Why doubt that, when it's always been a fact?

And when my problems start to multiply
I can't lose faith and start to question why.
He said for His name's sake that I would suffer.
Must run to Him; He'll be my Father buffer.

Whatever comes at me goes through Him first.
I am His child; my wounds He's always nursed.
And still I must protect my heart and mind.
Soft hearts need cover, like pineapple rind.

So I can keep out junk that isn't good,
Continuing to do just what I should,
God had to change my mind, and so my view.
Has God begun a good work too in you?

Crown

I cannot fight another round
I'm spent, fatigued, beat to the ground
My knees are weak, crushed by this weight
Is my call lost; is it too late?

With eyelids fat, I lay me down
Perhaps this isn't worth a crown
I know that I won't go to Hell
I'm sure that all of Heaven's swell

It's torture earning extra jewels
My sparkling crown beats those of fools
God knows I tried; I've done my best
So must I really pass each test?

I'm human; it can't be this hard
Or has my mindset left me marred?
I'm conscious of my slothful days
I must kick out rebellious ways

Fight when fatigued, sing when I'm sad
And then at judgment, I'll be glad
When knocked out, I did not stay down
I earned each jewel within this crown

Child of the King

We come into a sinful world, fallen as we are
But God will elevate our status, raise the bar
Beyond a splendor, we imagine we could see
Where King Eternal has decreed that we would be

> How can you make a difference in another's life
> If you let sharp-tongued comments slice you like
>   a knife?
> Now leave your pity party and embrace your call
> You're part of royal heritage; don't be thinking
>   small

> > *You are worthy, child; get your robe down*
> >   *from that shelf*
> > *Go on and put it on, girl; you better love*
> >   *yourself*

There is no lineage or gifts you need to bring
For God will elevate, equip you with all things
You're a regent here on Earth, endowed
    with what you need
So to fulfill your noble duties and succeed

> When will you grasp your legal, regal Family Line
> And discontinue your delay and waste of time?
> Lamenting like you're peasants, crying, "Oh,
>   poor me!"
> Now why do you deny that you are royalty?

You are chosen, child; get your scepter
    from that shelf
Go on and hold it firm, boy; you better
    love yourself

This kingdom has been given to you for doing good
Use your divine identity; do with it what you should
Hold out our royal scepter, so that others see
And lead your fellow countrymen to find their destiny

    You must claim that position, to fully walk
        within it
    And use your rank to rescue the oppressed
        from the pit
    Don't let improper mindset and lowly self-esteem
    Make you forget He died, so you could be
        redeemed

       You are capable, child; get your crown down
          from that shelf
       Go on and wear it proud, queen; you better
          love yourself

You can't be nervous when the devil raids your mind
As children of the King, you've got the power to bind
Bind up that liar, so he's not a hindrance
Use Jesus' name, and He must bow in reverence

    Be not beset by insecurity; be brave
    Think you're not worthy of the palace, so you cave
    Into the foul accuser's lies, who wants you pained
    When you are titled, you belong; you've
        been ordained

You are unstoppable, child; get your signet
    from that shelf
Go on and make your mark, king; you better
    love yourself

Don't listen to the serfs and opinions that they bring
When trusted chief advisors are waiting there
    with wings
Inherit your birthright; become a potentate
Now hold your head up high; don't walk askew
    but straight

The King has pre-ordained that you bring
    His realm glory
You've yet to have the crowning moment
    in your story
No, you're not ignorant, led blindly
    to the slaughter
It's time to rule and reign as the
    King's son and daughter

You are victorious, child; get yourself down
    from that shelf
Go now; sit on your throne, child; you better
    love yourself

Pass It On

Objective! Execute before we're gone
And take what God has done and pass it on

If operating other ways, it's half-witted
Trying to shove my way in places it's not fitted
I tried to do it solo, prove I need no one
But not a thing significant on my own was done

Forget "Army of *One*," and "Be all *you* can be"
Joint maneuvers with the five-star take priority
We're separate members, yes, but better as a whole
When working as a troop, we're really on a roll

Objective! Execute before we're gone
And take what God has done and pass it on

When we are linked with truth, there's power
     on our side
To wipe out vain imaginations like landslides
Bring thoughts into captivity; let people see us
Cast down high thoughts that try to rise above Jesus

So why do we divide in mind everything we do?
"This for God, this for me, and here's a bit for you."
Wait for your Commander; your orders are His will
Until you've your commands, ten-hut, stand fast,
     be still

Objective! Execute before we're gone
And take what God has done and pass it on

To earn a Purple Heart takes more than protocol
He'll leave the choice to us, to serve or go A.W.O.L.
Now forge ahead and charge against the
      dark foe's fort
Discharge your cannons all; hear the hot report

Blast the trumpets loud; there will be no shalom
Until the war is over, and you are safely home
Rout out all the foxholes; it's time now to engage
And have some thrilling stories to tell in your old age

Objective! Execute before we're gone
And take what God has done and pass it on

Also by Katherine Norland:

Poetic Prescriptions for Eternal Youth: *Examining Earthly Beauty from a Heavenly Perspective*

In this book, Katherine Norland picks apart societal standards of beauty that have been foisted upon us. She shatters misconceptions about image and self-worth in this truthful yet lighthearted look at our bodies and shows us the difference a divine perspective makes.

In *Poetic Prescriptions for Eternal Youth,* Katherine pops the fallacy of being perfect like a ripe zit, and lets her true self hang over the tight constraints of the media's portrayal of sexiness like a squishy muffintop over designer jeans a size too small.

She exposes the foibles she went through as a young woman, being bombarded by shapes in magazines she could never attain, then moves through the dread of aging when you no longer recognize yourself in the mirror, to embrace each new stage of life, cracks and all.

Although Katherine's self-esteem had been crushed like peanut shells at the corner bar, the transformation she found didn't come from a Beverly Hills plastic surgeon, but from shifting her perspective. She realized that a lasting makeover is not attained by starving yourself slim, Botoxing your brains out, or buying a Brazilian butt.

Instead of finding comfort in a candy bar, she began to examine earthly beauty from God's eyes, and in this book, she uncovers the real way to gain eternal youth.

Poetic Prescriptions for Plaguing Problems: *Biblical Remedies for When Life Bites*

Does your life bite?

You've gone to war in a flypaper dress, trying to catch each buzzing pest: those swarming problems that keep you from living the full life God has for you.

Does it seem like your prayers never get answered? Are you wondering where God is in all this?

This book of Bible-inspired poetry will assist you in finally terminating those plaguing problems, through God's help.

Made in the USA
Monee, IL
16 January 2021